Rumor of Hope

AD Poetry
Mills Lau

Mills, Laurel. Rumor of hope : poems
9001076737

Rumor of Hope

Poems by
Laurel Mills

Encircle Publications, LLC
Farmington, Maine

Rumor of Hope Copyright ©2012 Laurel Mills
Author/daughter photograph Copyright ©2005 Lynn Koss
Author photograph Copyright ©2011 Lynn Koss

ISBN-10 1-893035-16-6
ISBN-13 978-1-893035-16-4

All rights reserved. No part of this book may be reproduced in any form by any mechanical or electronic means including storage and retrieval systems without express permission in writing from the publisher. Brief passages may be quoted in review.

Editors: Cynthia Brackett-Vincent and Devin McGuire

Book design and cover design: Eddie Vincent/ENC Graphics Services

Cover photographs:
Sunset photograph Copyright © Keith Levit/shutterstock.com
Boat photograph Copyright © Doug Bennett/istockphoto.com

Printing: Walch Printing, Portland, Maine

Online Orders:
http://www.encirclepub.com/store/product/rumor-of-hope

Mail Orders, Author Inquiries:
Encircle Publications, LLC
P.O. Box 187
Farmington, ME USA 04938

Bookstores:
207-778-0467

Acknowledgements

The author wishes to acknowledge the editors of the following publications in which these poems appeared, some in slightly different versions:

The Anthology of New England Writers 2007: "Hands"

Wisconsin Academy of Sciences, Arts and Letters website: "Thinking of Beth as I Walk Among Flowers"

Wisconsin Review: "Every Breath Is Borrowed"

Contents

Thinking of Beth as I Walk Among Flowers 1
Parking Next to the Special Needs Pre-School. 2
How to Handle a Home Visit. 3
Dressing the Baby. 4
Camping at Hartman Creek 5
Easter Visit 6
Sometimes the Sun Forgets. 7
Mending My Daughter's Clothes 8
Riding the City Bus 9
Sheltered Workshop 10
Running Away 11
Baking Cookies. 12
Melody. 13
Hands. 14
Birds Falling from the Sky. 15
Every Breath Is Borrowed. 16
Reprieve, Again 17
Sisters Swimming 18
Paying It Forward 19
A Weekend Drive 20
Police Dog 21
The New *It Girl*. 22
The Imaginary Husband. 23
Cottage on the Chain of Lakes 24

About the Author. 25
A Note on the Poems 26

for
my lovely daughters,
Beth and Marissa

Thinking of Beth as I Walk Among Flowers

Ants find my doorstep, crawl through
the thin crack between door and sill.
I wonder if they've discovered the fragile
skull in the flowerbed—scattered paws,
bedraggled tail identify it as baby rabbit.
These things appear out of nowhere, yet
somehow I expect them. Like mushrooms
choking pansies in the whiskey barrel.
They weren't there yesterday; today
they spill over the edge.

I'm amazed by the lushness of this May
after two years of drought, one of spring
stammering its way back. All I can think
as I pull weeds from trailing dianthus
is *let me do the loving thing*. In brilliant
Sweet William I see blood that could spill
when Beth raises a fork to her roommate's back.
A year ago, I couldn't name her syndrome; now
it chokes out everything. What star decided
she should carry anger in her abdomen—
that it would rise and fall with each breath?

Aroma of honeysuckle, apple blossom nearly
fells me, reminds me of Beth's smile, so unexpected.
I hear her voice: *Me baby inside you?*
Yes, a quarter century ago.
I've given up asking why—I ride
with seasons. Rage will blossom,
but I hold onto her smile: sweet rosebud.

Parking Next to the Special Needs Pre-School

The ramp of the mini school bus lowers,
opens like a hand holding a gift,
presenting the girl to the special-needs teacher.
Watching, I think she seems all chair,
rubber padding for her wobbly head, footrests
her tiny legs don't reach, oversized wheels.
Inside the chair she is a pink bundle: pink snowsuit,
pink knit hat. The grandfatherly bus driver
pushes her onto the sidewalk, the March sun
glinting off the wheelchair, glinting off the girl's glasses.
The teacher and bus driver are smiling, their faces
wide with hope, their *good mornings* cheery.
They wheel her into the low brick building
with its modified blue and green swings, its huge
red balls flowering the yard. Watching them go,
watching the wide door swing closed behind them,
I remember when Beth was that age, when the little
yellow school bus carried her into her mornings—
when we thought we could change everything.

How to Handle a Home Visit

Slip bandages over her wrist
to keep her from picking
her own skin. Brush her hair
over the place where she dug
her scalp until it ran red.
Change her sanitary pad,
clean her ears with Q-tips,
running cotton over
the tender folds.
Wrap tape around
her middle toe where
she pulled off the nail,
flesh wrinkled and hot.
Change sheets in the bedroom
where last night she switched
the space heater to high.
Calm your heart as you
remove the seared blanket,
replace her charred pillow.

Dressing the Baby

For Beth's thirty-first birthday,
I buy baby clothes.
I help her fit the new diaper
around her doll's cloth bottom,
holding Edie's rubber legs
so Beth can slide on plastic pants.
We maneuver the arms
to slip the doll into pajamas.
Oh, Edie, Beth murmurs,
lifting the child to her shoulder.

Once, I imagined a real baby
in Beth's arms. My dream-eyes
saw the child's mouth
open into a smile,
saw downy fuzz on the head,
smelled milk breath.
Now I'm content with Beth's
tender humming, the pleasure
a cotton body gives her.

Later, I look in on Beth sleeping.
She rests soundly as if
her days were untroubled—
arms folded near her head
like wings, Edie tucked
into the blanket beside her.

Camping at Hartman Creek

We drive to the state park, raise our tent
in a pine grove, a layer of needles for a tarp.
Beth's cot goes in first, then she cozies her doll
on her sleeping bag. She is old enough
to tuck in a real baby, but she has taught me
to love this substitute grandchild.

Me no snore, Beth promises as she kisses
her doll goodnight. In the dark, pitch dripping
on our canvas roof, the tent will fill
with the uneven rhythm of my daughter's breathing:
small bursts, ceremonies of air.

Easter Visit

Beth searches her sister's apartment
for what the bunny left:
crayons, coloring book,
sugar-free gum in plastic eggs.
Throughout the day, she snitches
candy from a basket
hidden on Marissa's fridge,
denies it with chocolate mouth.

Dressing her doll in straw
bonnet, Beth asks for help
with the plastic shoes—
like the orthopedic ones
she wore thirty years ago
but never learned to tie.
Taking her hands, Marissa
guides the looping of the bow:
Make them like bunny ears, she says.

Later, they will color boiled eggs,
spread newspapers and pots
of dye on the kitchen table.
Writing with wax sticks
and dipping oval shapes
into yellow, blue, pink, lavender,
they will wait for the familiar
magic of their names.

Sometimes the Sun Forgets

We commit our children to this life,
to the stringing of day on day,
the building of years. If we were
to see the bare truth, would we ever
let those cells multiply
in the pelvic cradle of our bodies?
When Beth was an infant, we taped
a quarter to her navel. If only
all her wounds would heal so easily.
I could bargain my own death, chant
to the moon every fifth night,
cut crosses into my skin,
and still not change her story.
Sometimes the sun forgets her.
She crawls into darkness where we
can't find her behind fogged glass.
We see only her furious fingers
digging a roommate's cheek, her
hand jabbing at a friend's throat.
Yet we know: obscenities that spew
from her mouth are just the other side
of innocence. She doesn't mold them,
dry them in the kiln of her brain,
take them out tenderly, like a gift.
They rise from the sharp sparks
of neurons misfiring, escape before
she can trap them with her lips.
Even she is surprised by them.
Does it all come down to chemistry?
What formula would make her brain sing?

Mending My Daughter's Clothes

I remember my mother pulling
pins from pleats, tucking them
in her apron bib. Her graceful dance
of threaded needle
sewed dreams into the fabric
of my prom dress,
my blue commencement skirt,
hurried wedding gown.
We couldn't know then
that our dreams for Beth
would unravel. Over the years
of mending my daughter's
pajamas and sweatshirts,
I have learned to name
even the simplest stitch
embroidery.
As I prepare for her move
to yet another group home,
I stitch this prayer:
no more surprises.
Please, no night phone calls
that threaten to strap her down
in locked wards.
How much easier it was
to keep her safe
when we swaddled her
in blankets my mother crocheted.

Riding the City Bus

Beth doesn't like the bus—
too many people, too much noise.
She wants the bus to stop, wants to get off.

She fakes a seizure, throws her head back,
stiffens arms and legs, shakes her body
like a fish out of water, rolls her head.
The bus stops, she and her aide get off.

When she was two, Beth had a real seizure.
I heard thrashing in her crib, found
her little body in the grip

of something terrible. Muscles rigid,
twitching, jerking. Foam on her lips,
eyes rolled back. Then the limpness,
her lips blue, her skin translucent.

She fell into a sleep so deep that I
—so very, very young then—
feared she was dead.

Sheltered Workshop

Beth assembles plastic flip tops
for soda pop cans. Sometimes her hands
forget the task. She is drawn instead
to the man next to her, fascinated
with the hinge of his jaw, the way
breath makes skin puff and shrink.
If she could, she'd take his cheek,
carry that purse of muscle and tendon
in her fist. But the man's cheek
binds his sinus and bone. Without it
to resonate sound, he would be mute.
His skeletal face would stiffen and lock
and he could not say, *Don't touch me!*
The man is wary after weeks of working
beside Beth. He knows her hands might
fly up at any moment, homing pigeons
released in a storm. Even while
they are busy, he remembers
the sharp peck, the beaks of fingernails.

Running Away

Last week my daughter wandered
from her group home, away from
the blue house with its aroma of stew
and the prattle of her friends. She walked
away from the aide who was her keeper,
out the door, past hanging pots of pink azalea,
down the long sloping driveway toward
the busy road at the bottom of the hill.
When she walked into the line of traffic,
cars whizzing by in both directions,
a cardinal was singing and chicory lined the roadside.
And when the police car came, the sun shone
in a sky that was unblemished and pure—
not one hint of the dangers in the world.

Baking Cookies

I roll dough. Beth stamps out
stars, pine trees, and Santas,
then licks her sticky fingers.
I slide the pan into a hot oven,
let her close the door.

We listen to the radio playing
Rockin' Around the Christmas Tree
while we wait for cookies to bake
so we can spread frosting
and sprinkle colored sugar.

Beth says, *I luf you, Mom.*
No gift is sweeter: red-and-green apron
high on her waist, flour on her cheek,
words that waited these many years
to spill from the bell of her tongue.

Melody

Whenever Beth talks, the words
are halting, never fully formed
in the chamber of her mouth,
refusing to roll off her stubborn tongue.
Tonight, my friend strums a guitar,
pure notes trilling from her lips as she sings
Christmas carols and folk music.
Beth plunks on her own guitar,
and occasionally she croons out a word
from songs she's heard so often
the melody sparks memory.
This is *music*—that marvel—
a mezzo soprano singing sweetly
and Beth joining in at the end
of a line, her pitch almost true.

Hands

The back seat is full of opened Christmas gifts
—flannel pj's, plastic nurse's kit, pink-wrapped doll—
as I drive my grown daughter to her group home.
Country music thumps on the radio, Beth
snapping her fingers slightly off the beat.
Rounding a curve, my car loses power and dies.
Beth cries, *Oh no, me have heart attack!*

I bundle her up, and we plod arm-in-arm
to a building on the edge of this unfamiliar town.
Inside, people are celebrating the season:
a tree with colored lights, long tables set for dinner.
A man in blue jeans offers to help us
and reaches for his cell phone.

How to keep Beth's hands
away from presents under the tree,
out of bowls of stuffing and mashed potatoes?
In the back of the hall, reverent voices pray
Thank you for this food… while the man
tries to locate a service station on a holiday weekend.

Beth has no place for her hands.
I deflect a grab towards a woman's black purse,
but I'm not fast enough to keep her
from reaching for the man's crotch,
the soft bulge in denim. He dances away
like someone dodging a dog's inquisitive nose.

Quickly, I encase Beth's fingers in thick mittens,
hurry her out into the cold winter air, holding
her blizzard of hands while we wait for the tow truck.

Birds Falling from the Sky

On New Year's Eve in Arkansas,
5,000 redwing blackbirds and starlings
plummet from the heavens. Simply
rain down, littering a town
with featherweight bodies, wings
outstretched, rigid legs skyward.

Days later 500 blackbirds, starlings, grackles
litter a Louisiana highway, dark
carcasses on the road, on the shoulder,
in drainage ditches as motorists speed past,
flattening birds in the roadway.

In Italy, hundreds of turtledoves fall
lifeless from the sky, their grey bodies
scattered in the streets, in flower beds,
hanging from trees. In Sweden,
over a hundred jackdaws
are found dead on a snow-covered street.

This winter, Beth falls headfirst
down a flight of basement stairs, hurtling
though space, following gravity's pull.
They find her face down,
slammed against the concrete floor.

In the ICU hospital bed at Mercy,
my daughter looks like a broken bird.
Her eyes, black as raven's wings.
Her head: cracked eggshell in its nest of pillows.

Every Breath Is Borrowed

My daughter sleeps in the summer sun,
lying full-length in a little valley of grass.
Her sleep is deep, too deep for this bright afternoon.
She looks like a holocaust victim, her face
tea-stained parchment, thin and drawn.
Her arms and legs
purpled with bruises from falls,
red with sores where she has bitten herself.
Wrapped in the fog of anti-psychotic drugs,
she's losing all the hard-earned skills:
how to dress herself, how to flush the toilet.
At forty she's becoming senile, wearing diapers.
Before I found her out here, she'd told me, *I'm cold.*
Only lying in the sun seems to warm her.
The chimes on the patio make a tinkling song,
pink geraniums in clay pots are fully blossomed.
Is she breathing? I wonder
and wiggle her toe to see if she wakes.
She stirs, gurgles like a baby, groans.
Breathe deep, I want to say.
The neighbor's colorful sheets hang like flags
on the line. Water bubbles
in the fake waterfall on our patio.
Is she practicing her death, all the years
she'll sleep under a blanket of grass?
In one tender moment—I swear this is true—
a monarch butterfly, orange with black hem,
flits near her head. Under the landscape of the sun,
it lands briefly on her forehead.

Reprieve, Again

The doors are locked where she is:
heavy metal doors, an aide
with a jangle of keys on her belt.
Beth is being weaned off Haldol,
Risperdal, clonazepam, lorazepam, Buspar.
Only Seroquel remains to quiet
the attack dog in her belly.
Things are coming back to her—
how to dress herself, chew food,
how to turn on the TV and watch
her favorite bowling show.
How to make X's and numbers
and *keep score*. She claps and shouts
all right! when pins tumble
and spin into the dark void behind.
She watches balls speed down slick lanes,
the way asteroids hurtle through space,
and when the pins are sent flying,
she's happy for the wild luck of it all.

Sisters Swimming

When Beth swam in my maternal bowl
—carried in the cradlebones—
the fluid wasn't right. Three years later,
Marissa tread that water safely.

As toddlers, they bathed together
in a clawfoot tub. Once, Marissa
convinced Beth to drink shampoo,
marveled at the shimmery bubbles she spit.

When we lived in the valley of the Adirondacks,
nothing could keep Beth out of frigid Lake George.
Her sister, in a more cautious stage, waited,
wrapped in a white towel, on the pine-edged shore.

One summer Beth, in wool cardigan, slipped off
the dock at Moosehead, her plastic baseball cap
marking the spot. The next year Marissa, dragging
a bucket, walked off the pier at Lake Winnebago.

There were vacations at Dummer's Beach, wading
the shallow water back-dropped by mountains,
stirring up mica. On Lake Michigan the girls huddled
in a yellow raft, riding the wake behind our cabin cruiser.

Now they are grown, with Marissa lifeguard
and caretaker. Whenever they go swimming,
Beth says, *Me no dive!* and will not jump in.
But Marissa assures her, *We'll do it together.*

They make the plunge. When their heads emerge
from that bowl of blue water, all around them:
scattered rainbows, little prisms of light.

Paying It Forward

On the farmland trail where
his aunts taught him
to ride a bike, the boy,
now sixteen, is helping
Beth as she struggles
to keep her adult tricycle
on the gravel path. Grasshoppers
pop at his ankles, chipmunks scurry
from hiding place to hiding place.
The boy's running is easy and natural
as he races beside Beth,
his hands gripping one handlebar
to keep her from drifting.
When she heads for the ditch,
crying, *Emergency, emergency!*
he guides her back to the trail.
For half a mile, she pedals
and he runs beside her.
Then they stop for what she calls
a break of water and granola.
Turning, they retrace their steps,
the autumn sun glinting
off corn tassels and feathery grasses
as the bike wheels spin,
the long circle repeating itself.

A Weekend Drive

Beth settles her doll into the back seat. She pulls
a seatbelt across the belly, the rubber arms.
There, Edie, she says, *safe*.
Then she buckles herself beside her baby.
As I slip into the driver's seat, I watch her
sneak a glance at herself in the rearview mirror,
see the asymmetrical grin, the wink
she gives her reflected face. Perhaps
she's learning, at forty, to love herself.
In the mirror I see her smile—mouth bluish
with eye shadow from the tube she mistook for lipstick.
She turns to her doll, patting the cloth tummy.
Good girl, Edie, she says.

Police Dog

In her room at the group home, Beth
watches reality police shows, the refrain
bad boys, bad boys repeating

in her head. She's Cop Woman, cocking
her finger at the TV screen, blowing
a puff of air across the tip of her revolver.

She admires K9 dogs who detect evil.
In the mall with her friends and an aide
She's Police Dog, sniffing the crowd for danger.

A man coming toward them, carrying shopping bags,
seems a threat. Beth bends from the waist, not quite
on all fours, bares her teeth and barks.

Grrr, grrr, a throaty growl. *Grrr!*

The man steps back out of the way, surprise
furrowing his face, as Police Dog Beth,
her friends, and aide pass safely by.

The New *It Girl*

She wears her forties like a good dress,
jaunty and swinging in the breeze.

Her hair's in a ponytail, done up
in ribbons by her group home staff.

She's into makeup—green eye shadow,
blue nail polish, rouge on the cheekbones.

She's got her tennis racket, bowling bag,
her ticket to the movies, money for popcorn.

She's carrying a pink plaid purse, her
Walkman and headphones. She's got

music to go and a guitar at home.
She's got jazz, pizzazz, razzmatazz.

She's riding a three-wheel bike
with a pink flag. In the basket, her baby doll.

The Imaginary Husband

The ring on her finger is the size of Texas, plastic,
red and blue, a lone star from the vending machine.
My wedding ring, she says. *Bob, my husband.*
When asked to give Bob's last name,
she looks away and shrugs. *I dunno.*
Maybe this is her fantasy life: she has a dog
and two cats. The cats' names are Fluffy and Nutty.
The dog is a Brittany spaniel and sleeps on their bed
at night near Bob's feet. The dog stirs
when Bob shifts to wrap his arm around Beth.
When the sun comes up, Bob kisses Beth
on the fragile line of her collarbone.
He makes scrambled eggs with shredded
cheese and shallots; she makes cinnamon toast.
They eat on the front porch and wave
to the paper boy when he bicycles past.
All day at the sheltered workshop
Beth thinks of Bob and plans their supper.
They like to do the dishes together,
though they argue about who washes and who dries.
They tell about their day, all the little gossips.
Fluffy and Nutty meow around their legs, the dog
waits for a walk around the block when Bob and Beth
will *howdy* at neighbors. They take their coffee
to the little garden at the back of the house.
Bob nips the dried geranium; Beth pulls a thistle
from the nasturtiums. Curled on the brick patio,
dreaming of rabbits, the dog farts in his sleep.
This is the story of their life together, the story of
Mr. and Mrs. I-Dunno and their very ordinary days.

Cottage on the Chain of Lakes

We sit in Adirondack chairs,
sipping coffee and hot chocolate,
watching a hummingbird—tiny green angel—
flit near a globe of red sugar water.
Beth has come back from six months
under lock and key. She's quiet,
feeling her way back into the raucous world.
The great blue sky, chipmunks scurrying
in pine needles under the picnic table—
these are new wonders to her again.
Each green leaf moving in the breeze
is a small blessing.

We decide to take the canoe out,
to venture into unknown water.
From the middle seat, in orange life jacket,
Beth says, *Boat hole*, pointing
to a railroad trestle over the creek
that feeds this small lake.
We veer in that direction, paddling
under the bridge to the other side
where the water is shallow.
A great blue heron, knee deep,
watches cautiously on stick legs
as we glide by. We can see below
to stones that glitter in the sun.
Weeds wave and sway in the river
like a rumor of hope.

About the Author

Author Laurel Mills was born in Wilton, Maine, and lives in Neenah, Wisconsin. She is the author of four award-winning poetry chapbooks, including *Hidden Seed*, which was published in Troika IV by Thorntree Press and won the Posner Poetry Award. Laurel is Senior Lecturer Emerita at the University of Wisconsin-Fox Valley, where she taught English and edited the literary magazine *Fox Cry Review*. To contact the author, visit her website: www.laurelmills.net.

Laurel's daughter, Beth Mills, who has the rare genetic condition 1p36 Deletion Syndrome, lives in a group home run by Empowerment Living Services and works at Lakeside Packaging Plus, a sheltered workshop. She enjoys bowling, swimming, biking, eating out, going to movies, and listening to music.

A Note on the Poems

1p36 Deletion Syndrome is a rare genetic condition in which material is missing from the end of chromosome one. This deletion typically causes intellectual disability and a number of other characteristics; in about half of the individuals, the syndrome causes behavior disorders. To learn more, visit 1p36 Deletion Support & Awareness website at http://www.1p36dsa.org.